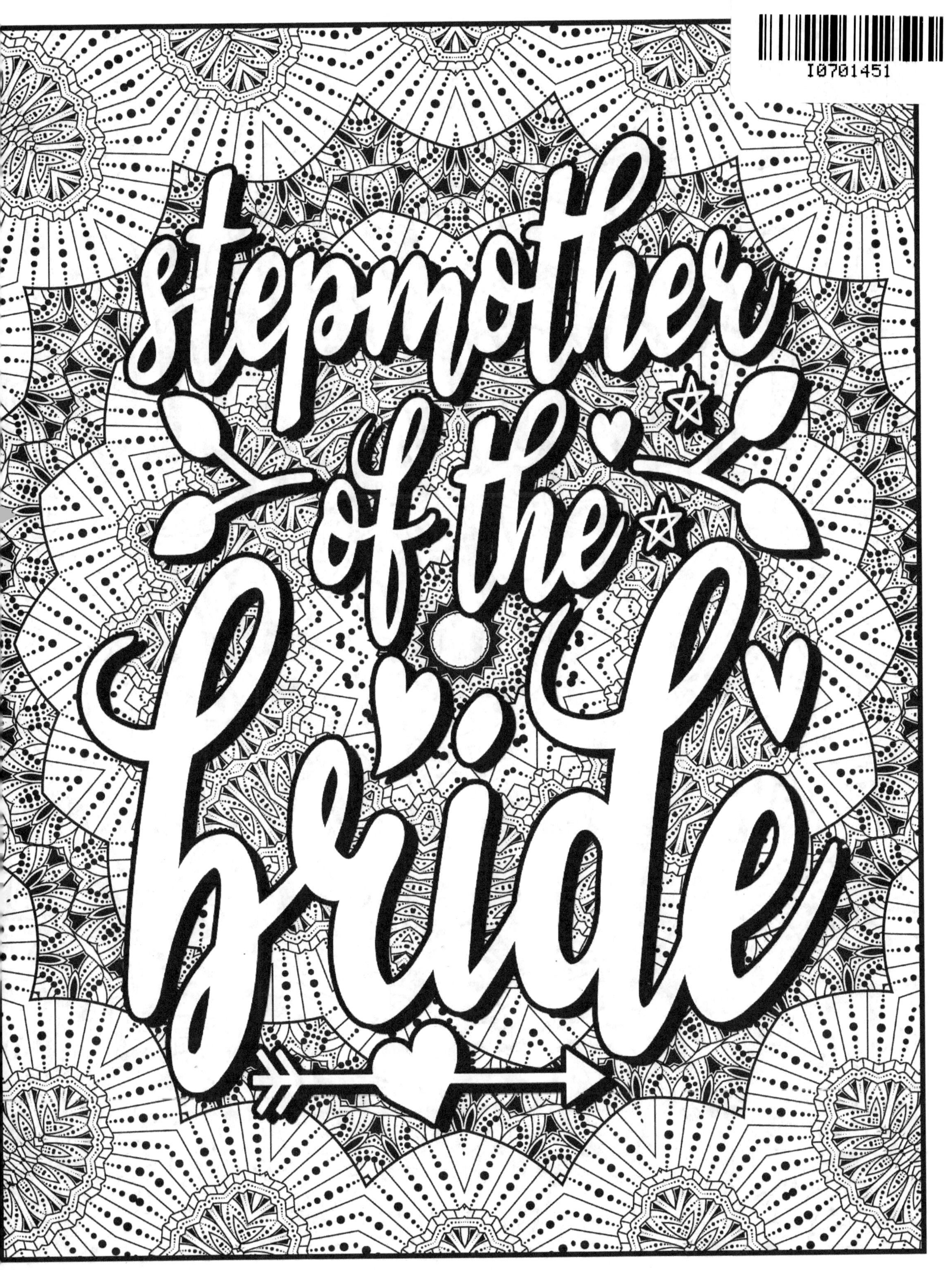

stepmother
of the
bride

Thankful
for my
Tribe

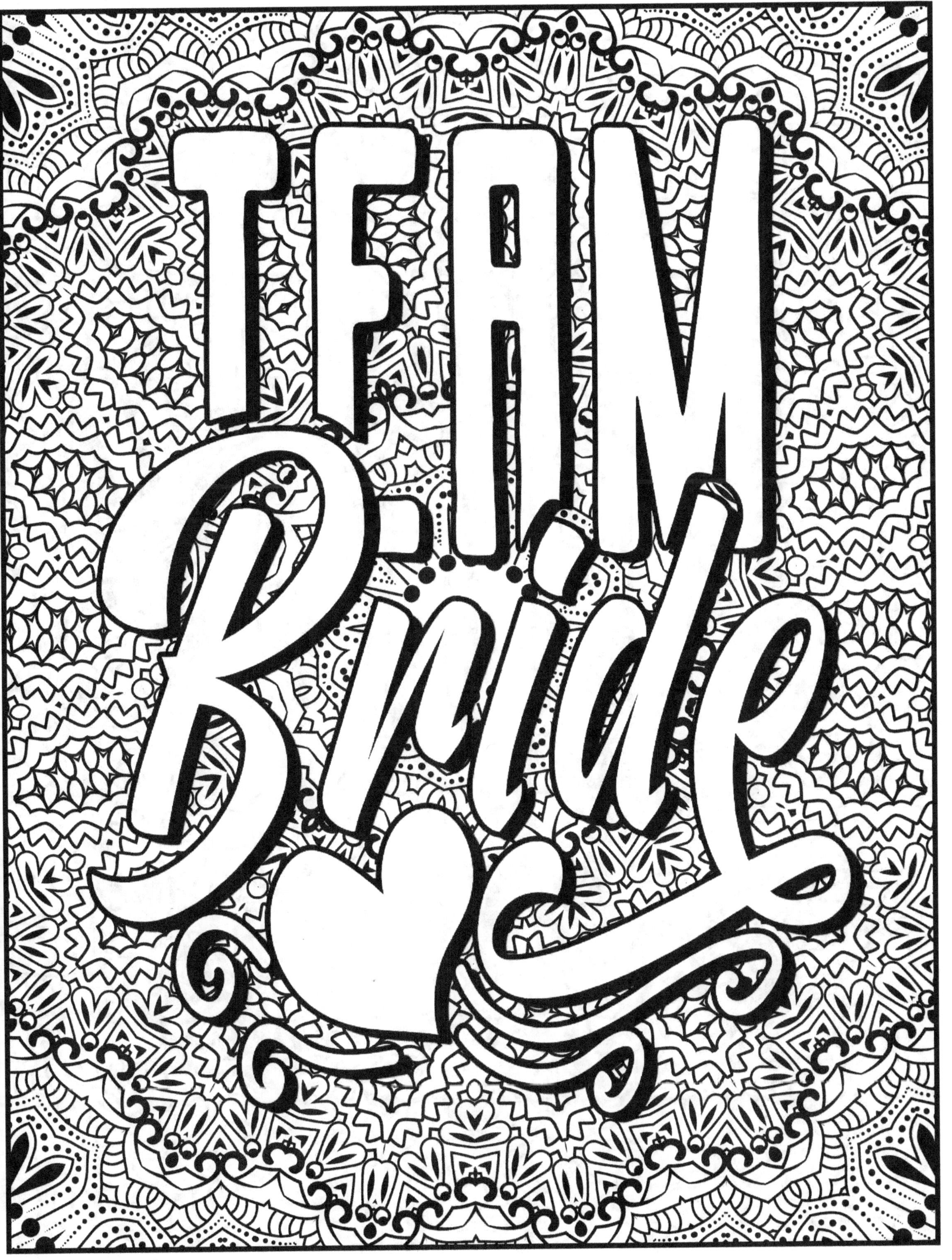

TEAM
Bride

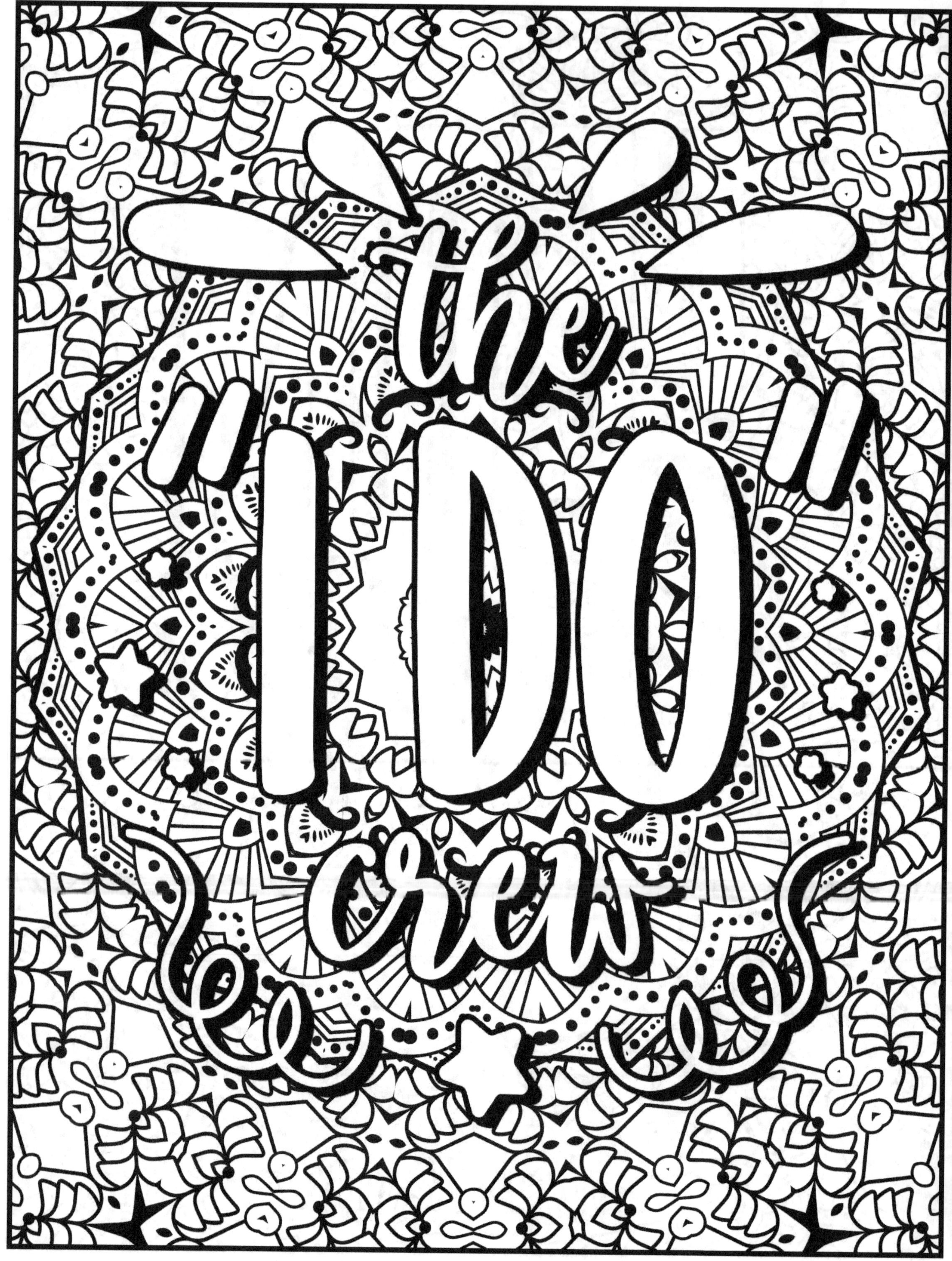

the
"I DO"
crew

thankful
for my
TRIBE

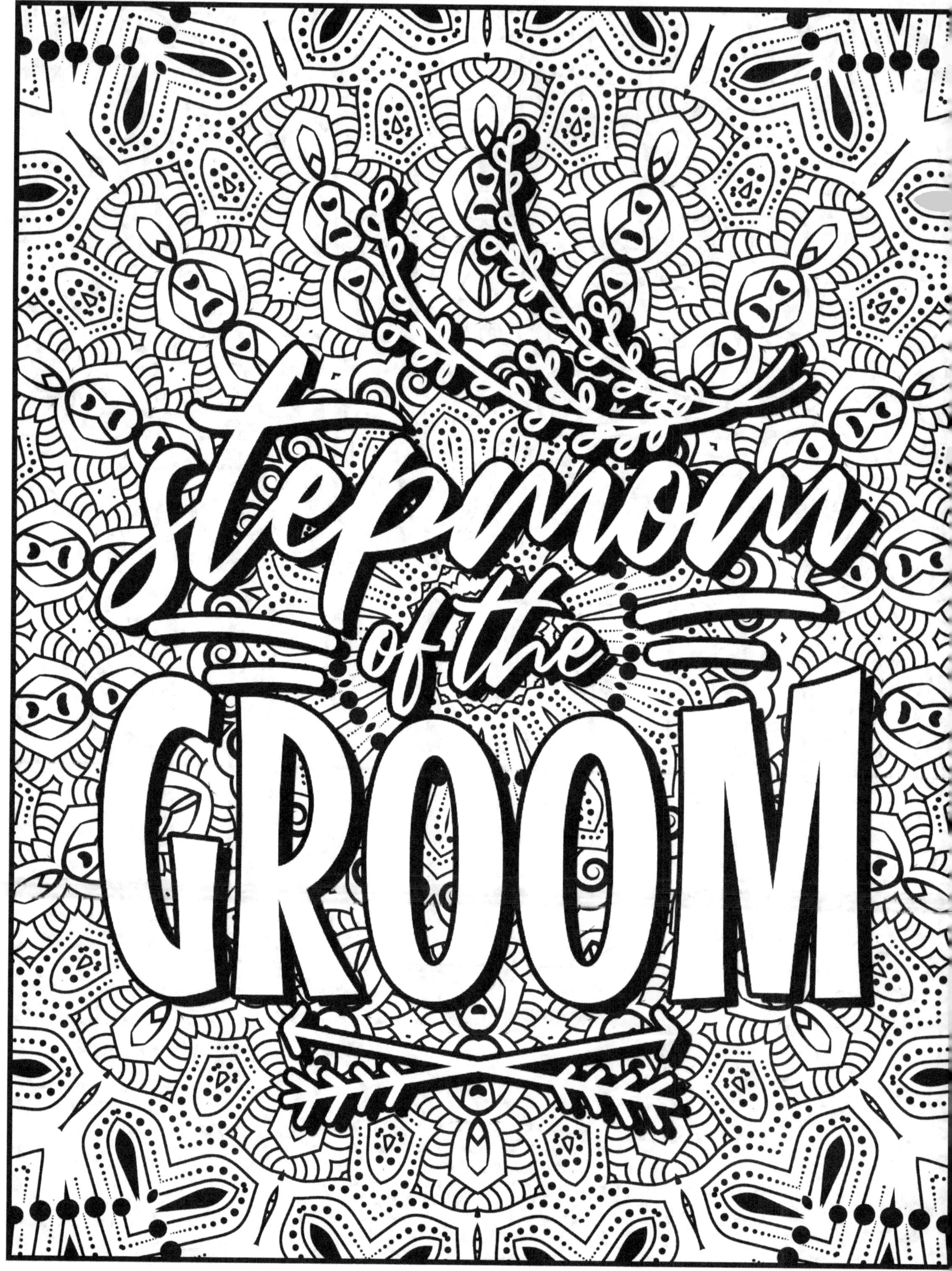

stepmom
of the
GROOM

Sweating
for the
Wedding

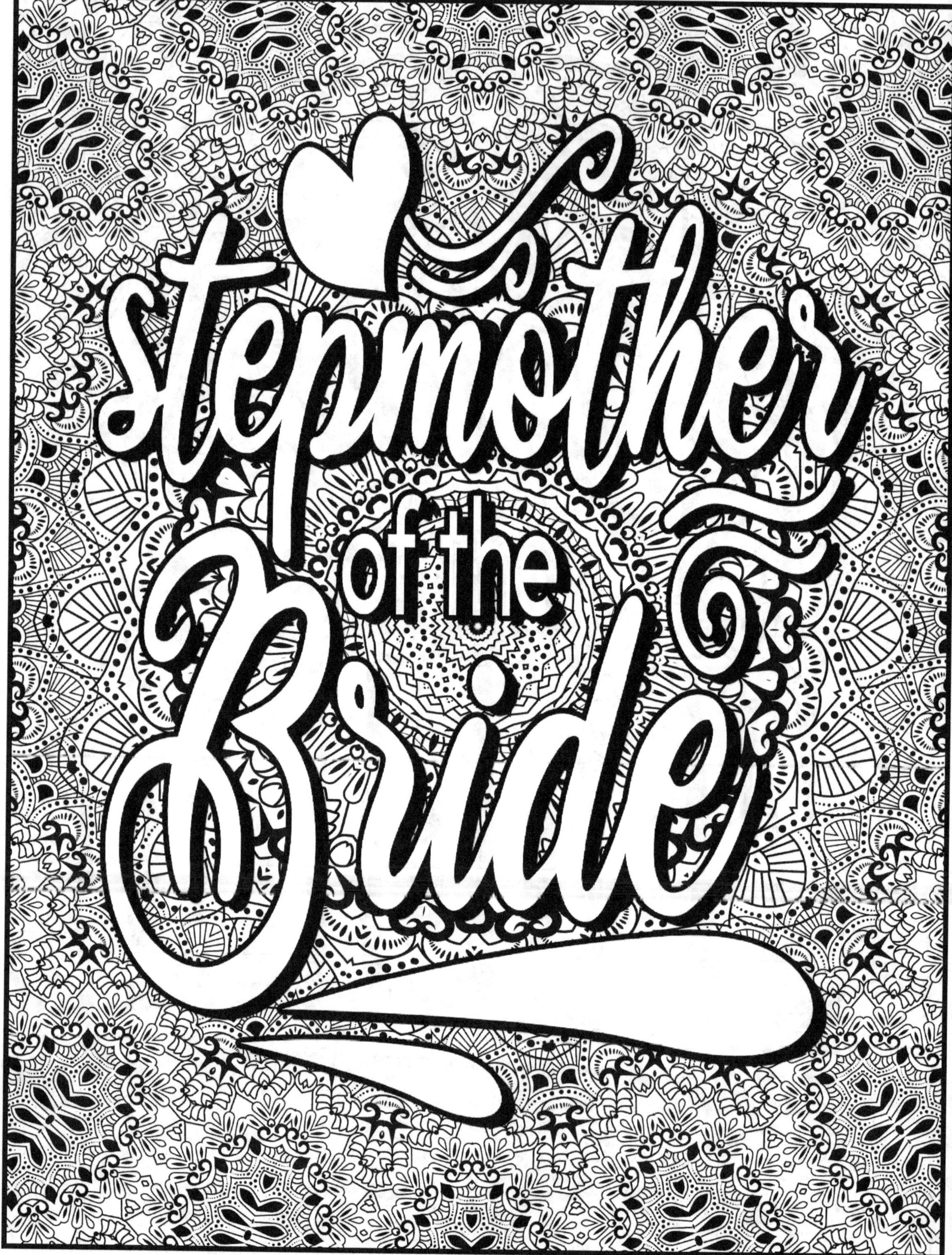

stepmother
of the
Bride

Sweating
for the
WEDDING

stepmother
OF THE
GROOM

STEPMOM
of the
Bride

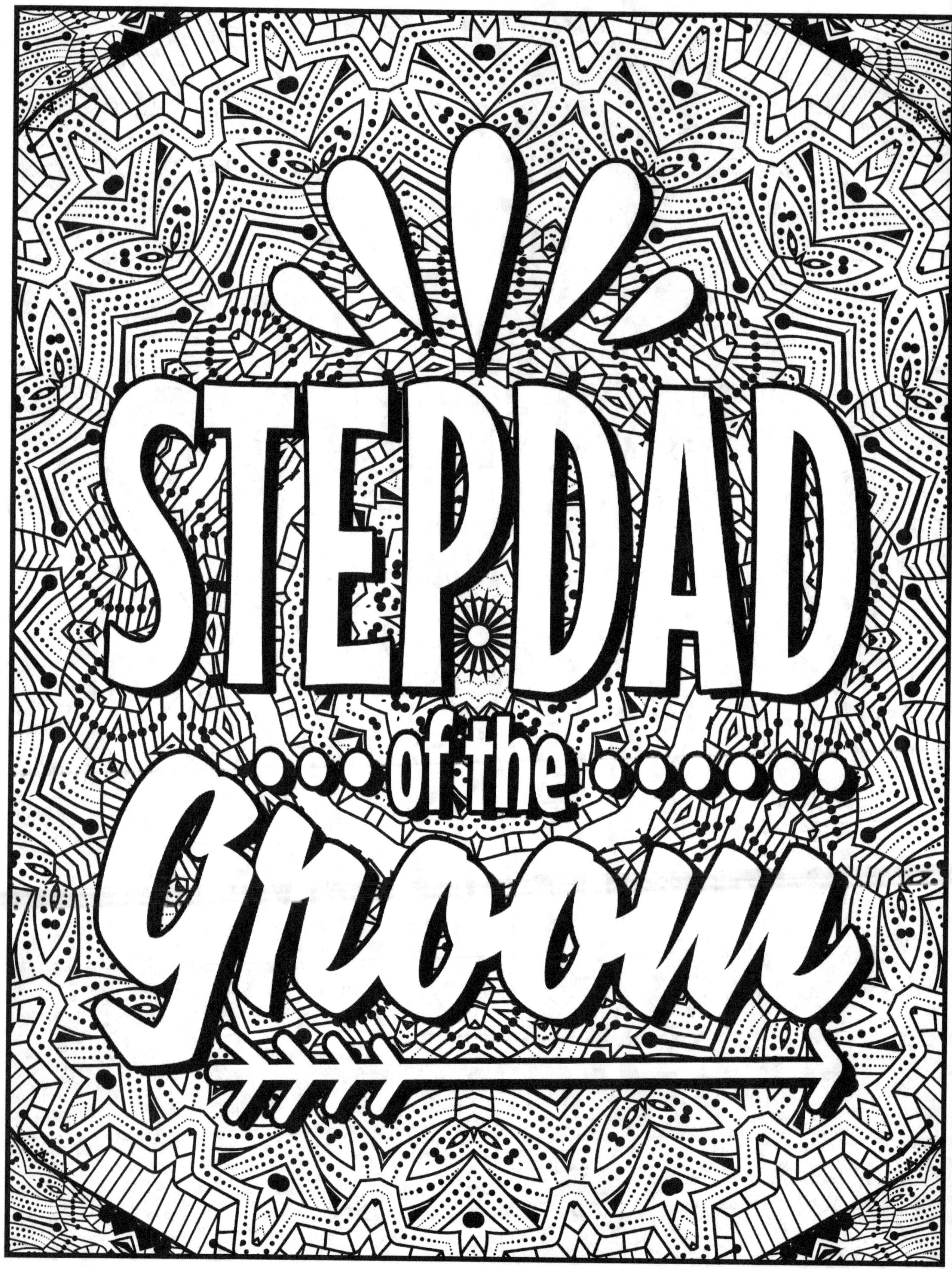

STEP DAD
of the
groom

ring
bearer

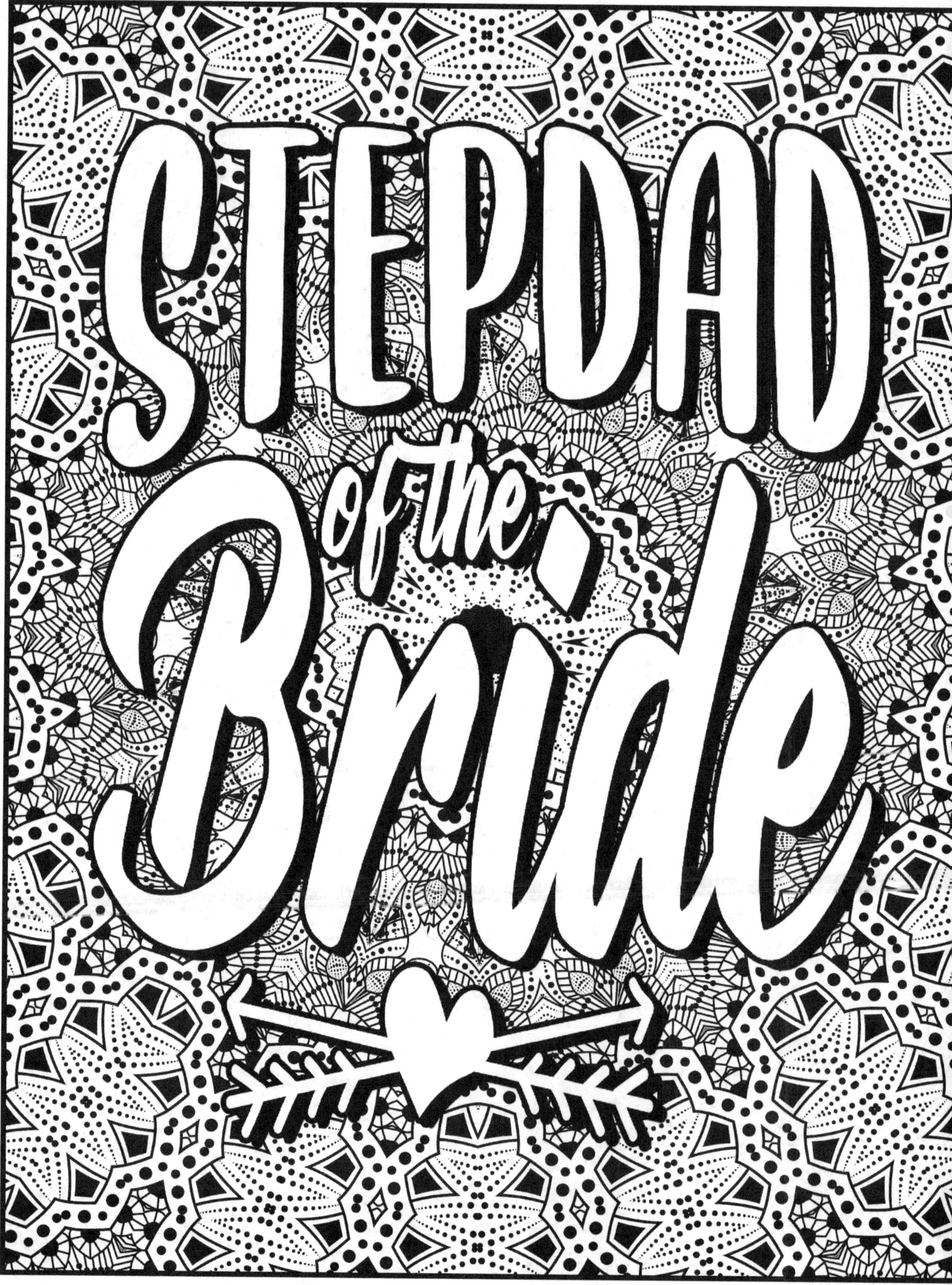

STEPDAD
of the
Bride

Ring
SECURITY

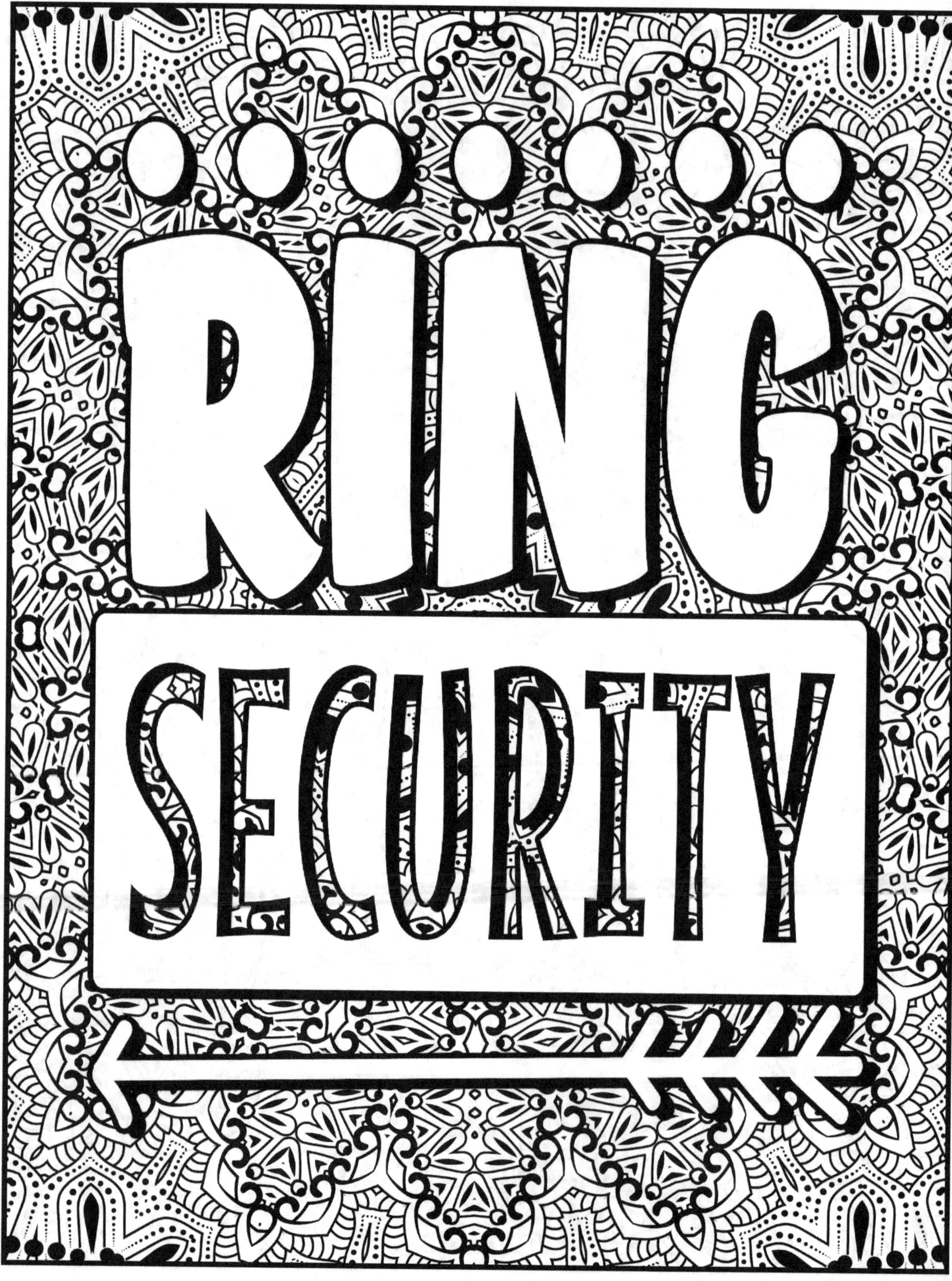

RING
SECURITY

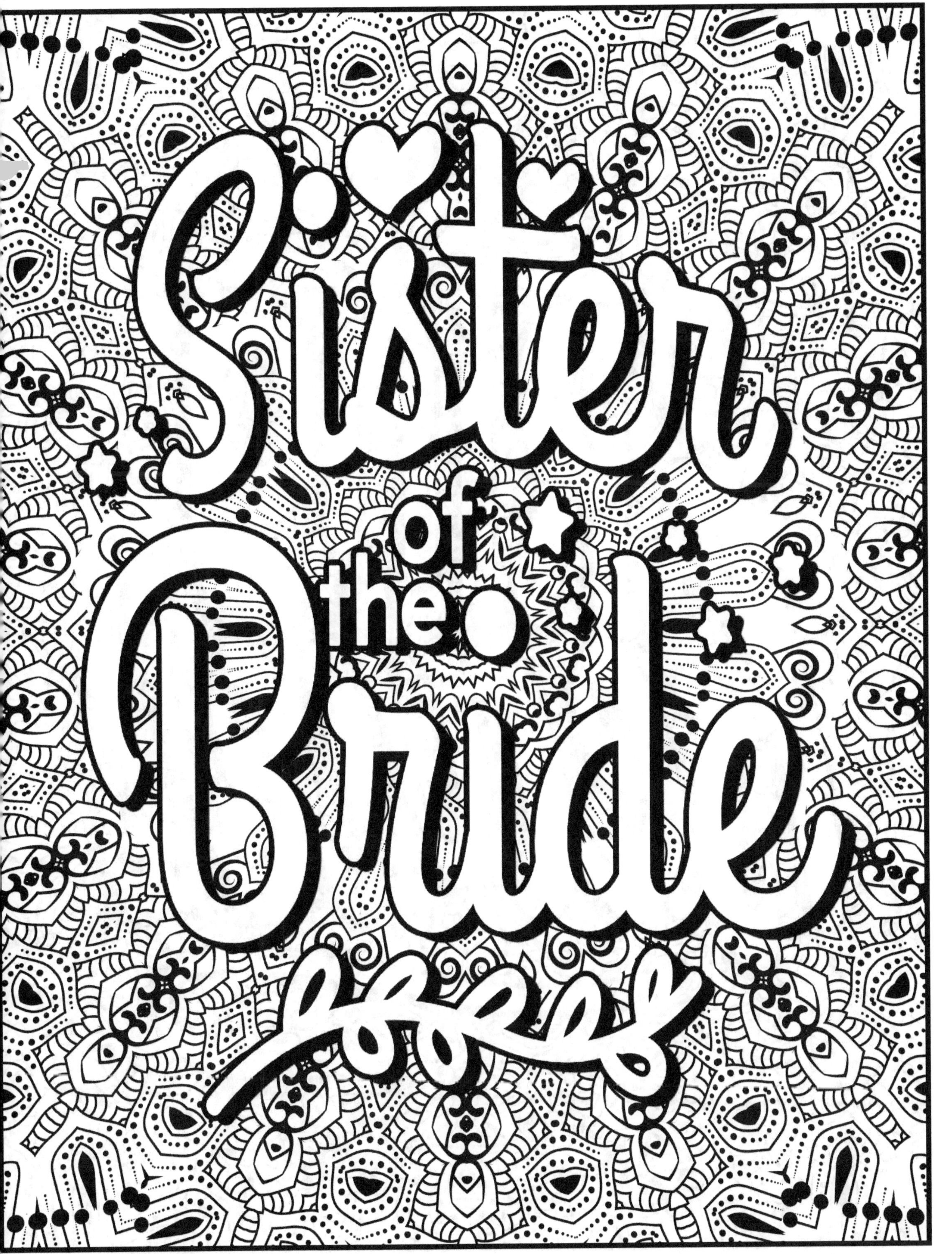

Sister
of
the
Bride

Ring
Bearer

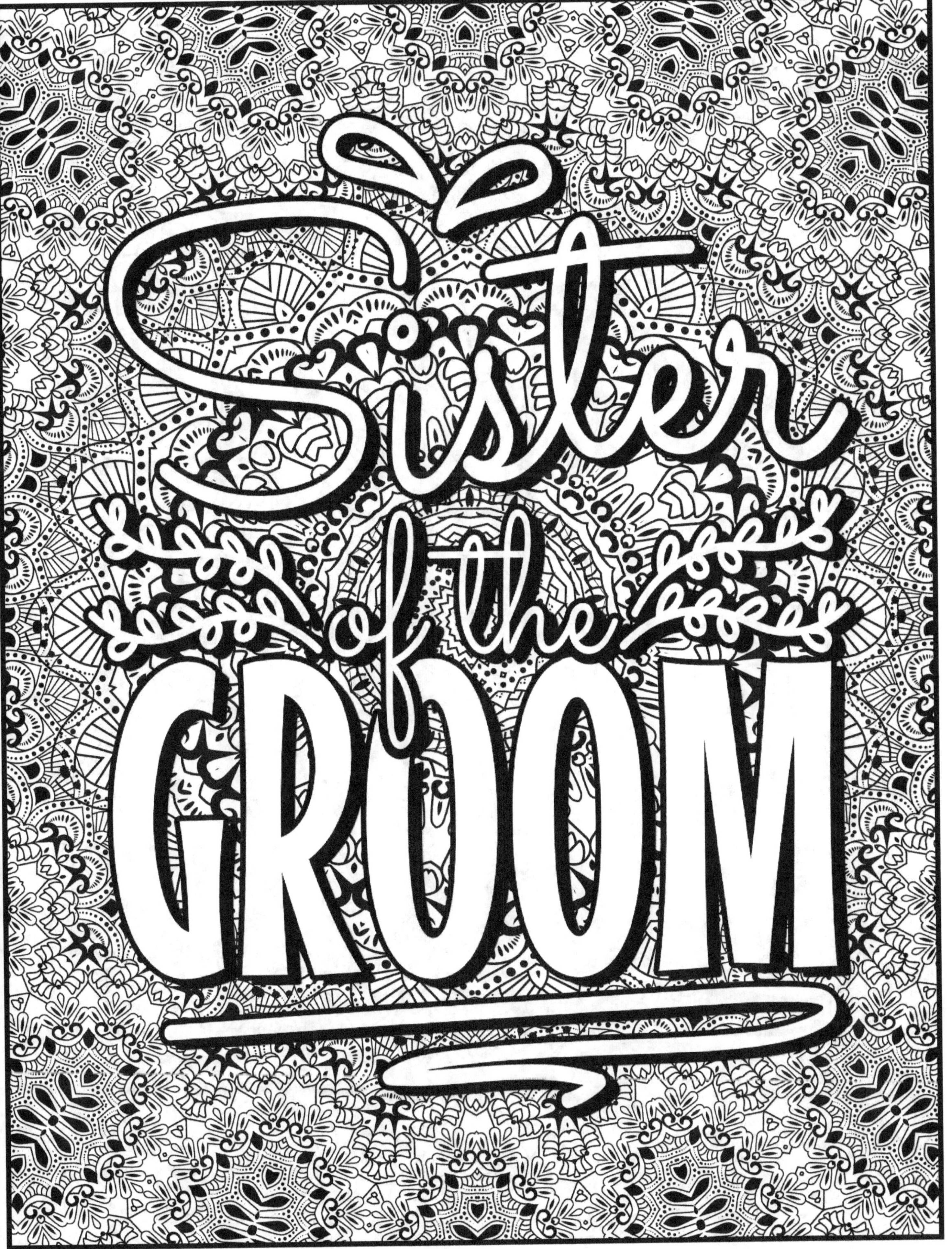

Sister
of the
GROOM

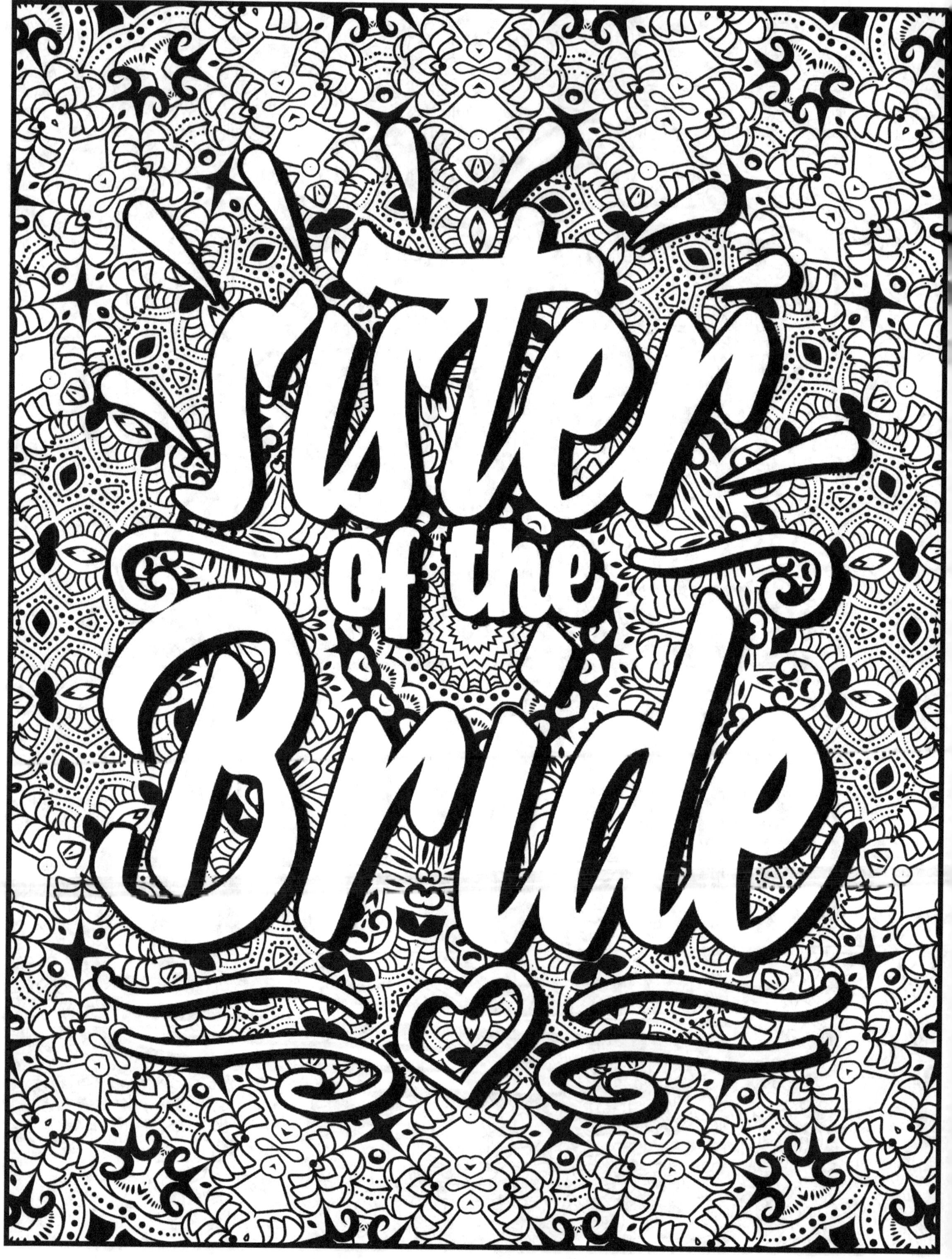

Sister
of the
Bride

Sister
OF THE
GROOM

son
of the
bride

Son
of the
GROOM

WILL YOU
BE MY
matron
OF HONOR

will you
be my
matron
of honor

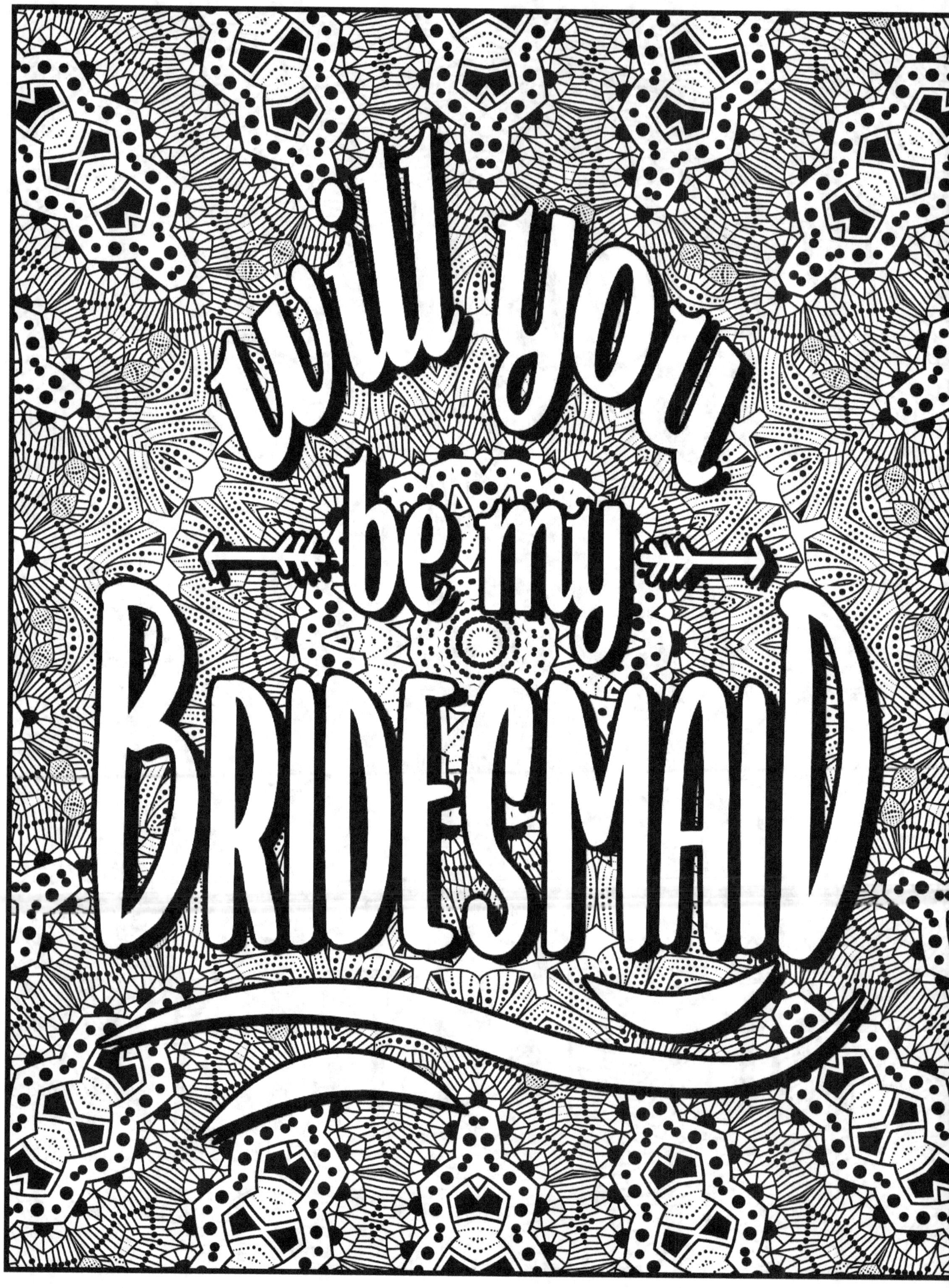

will you
be my
BRIDESMAID

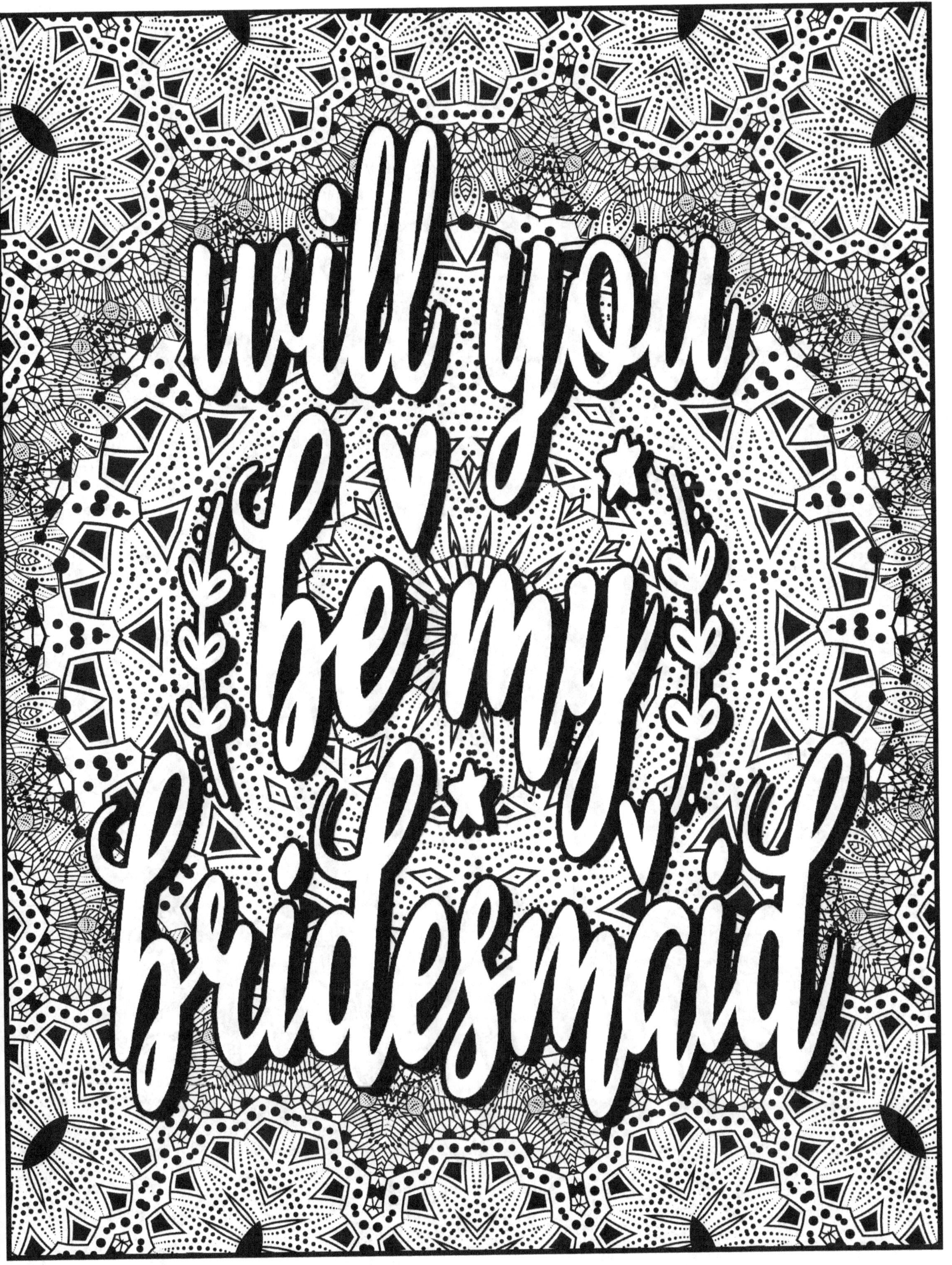

will you
be my
bridesmaid

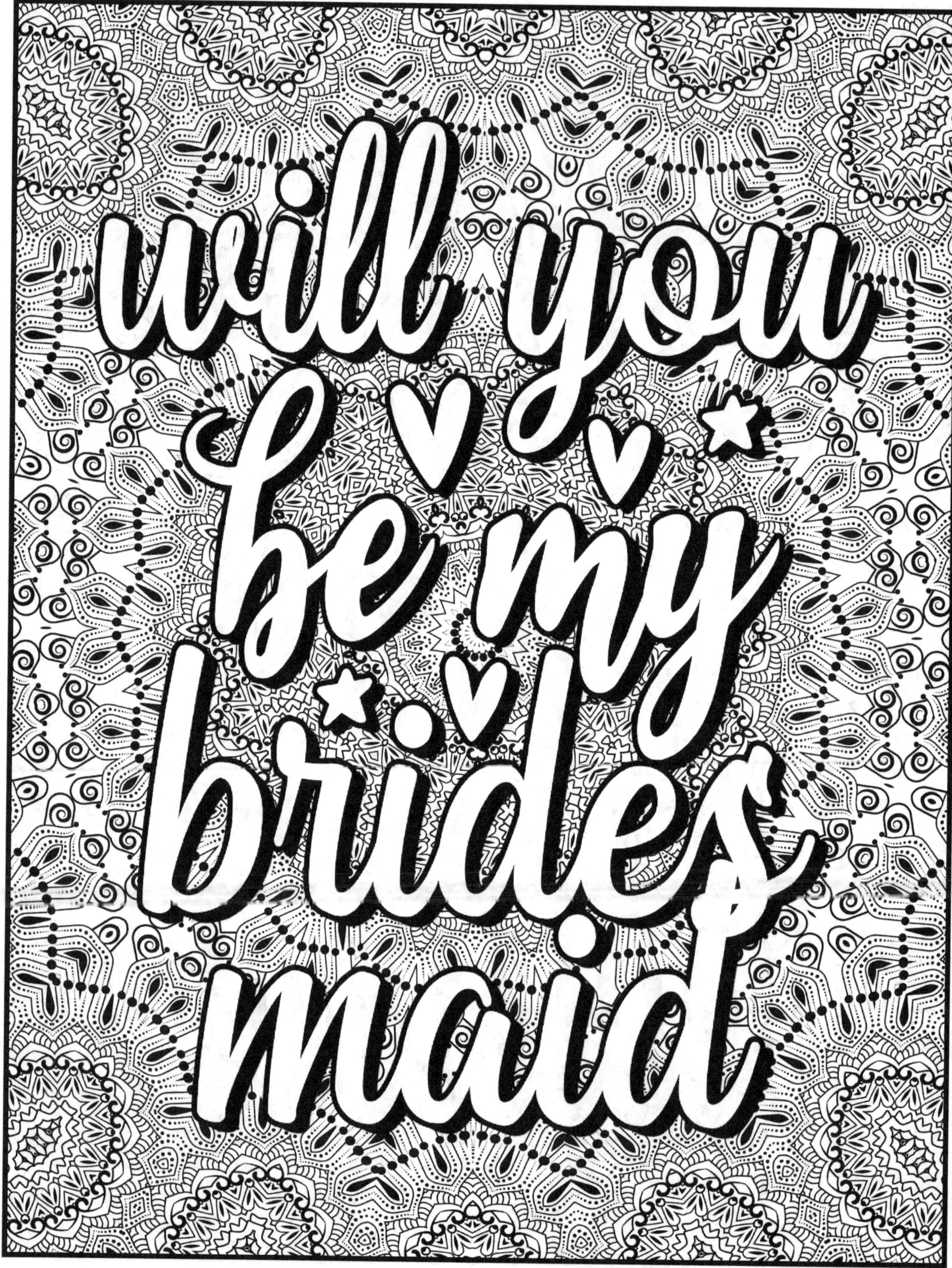

will you
be my
brides
maid

will you
be my
bridesmaid

WERE
engaged

we're
ENGAGED!

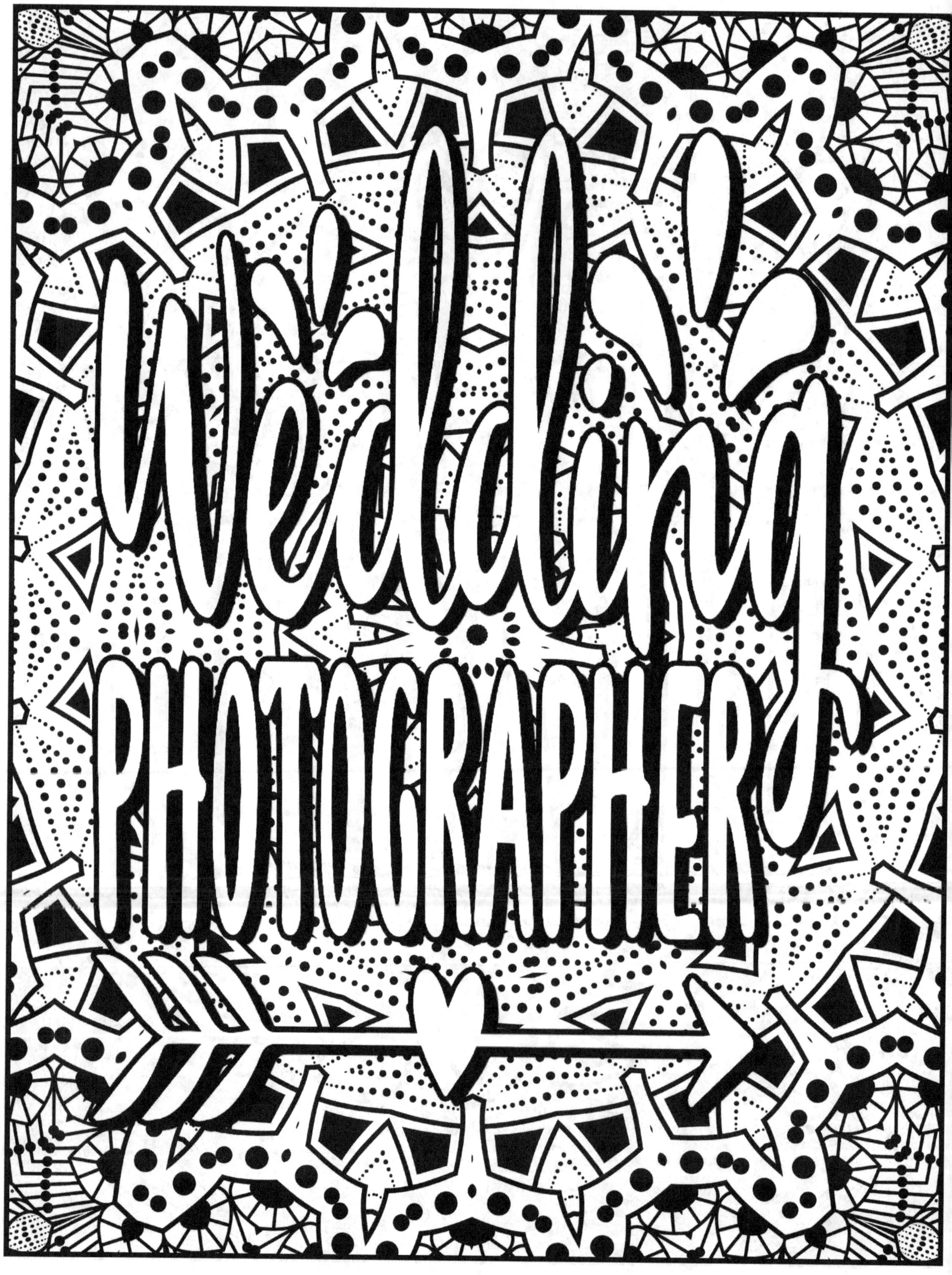

Wedding
PHOTOGRAPHER

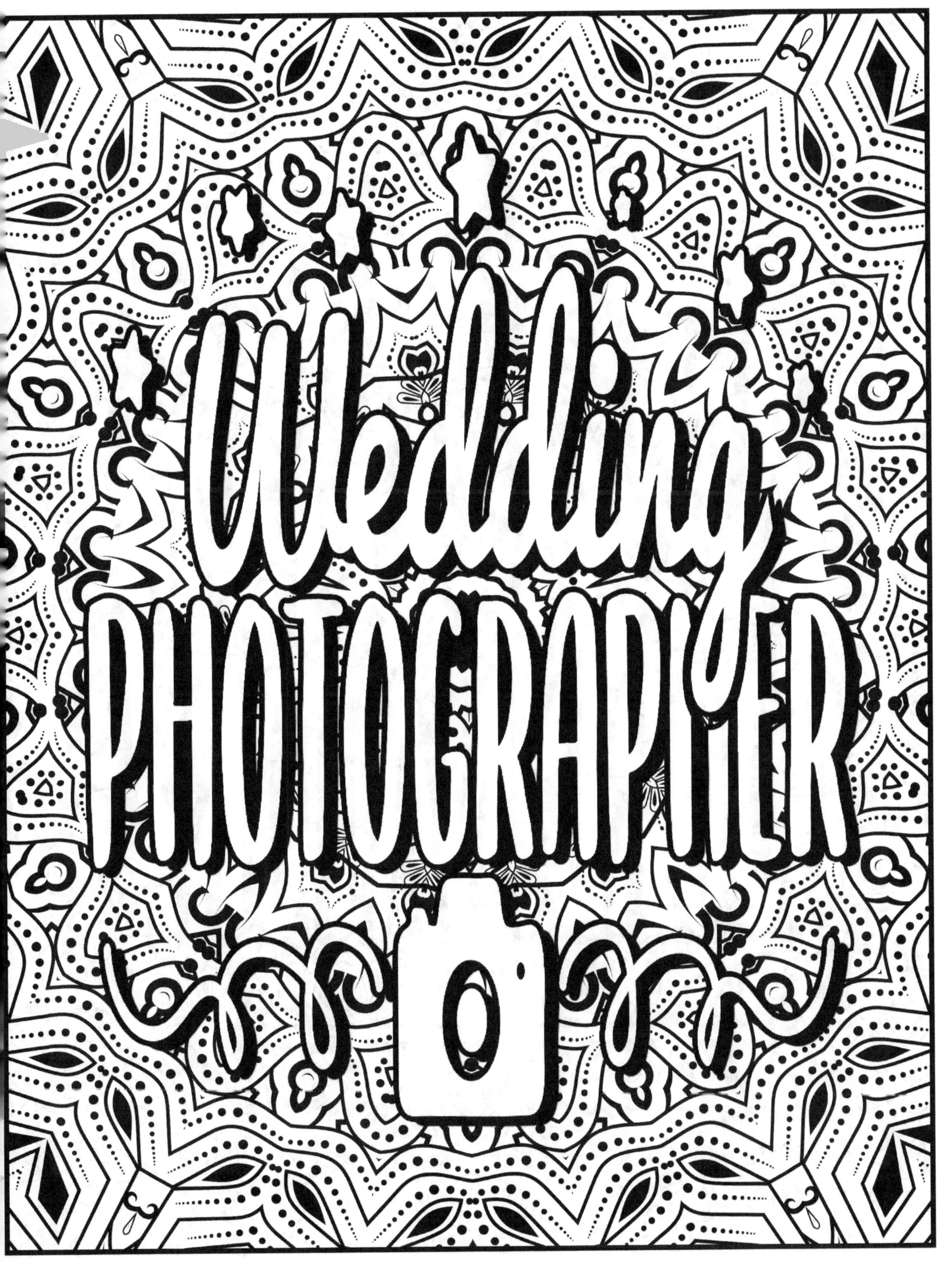
Wedding
PHOTOGRAPHER

Wedding
COORDINATOR

Wedding
COORDINATOR

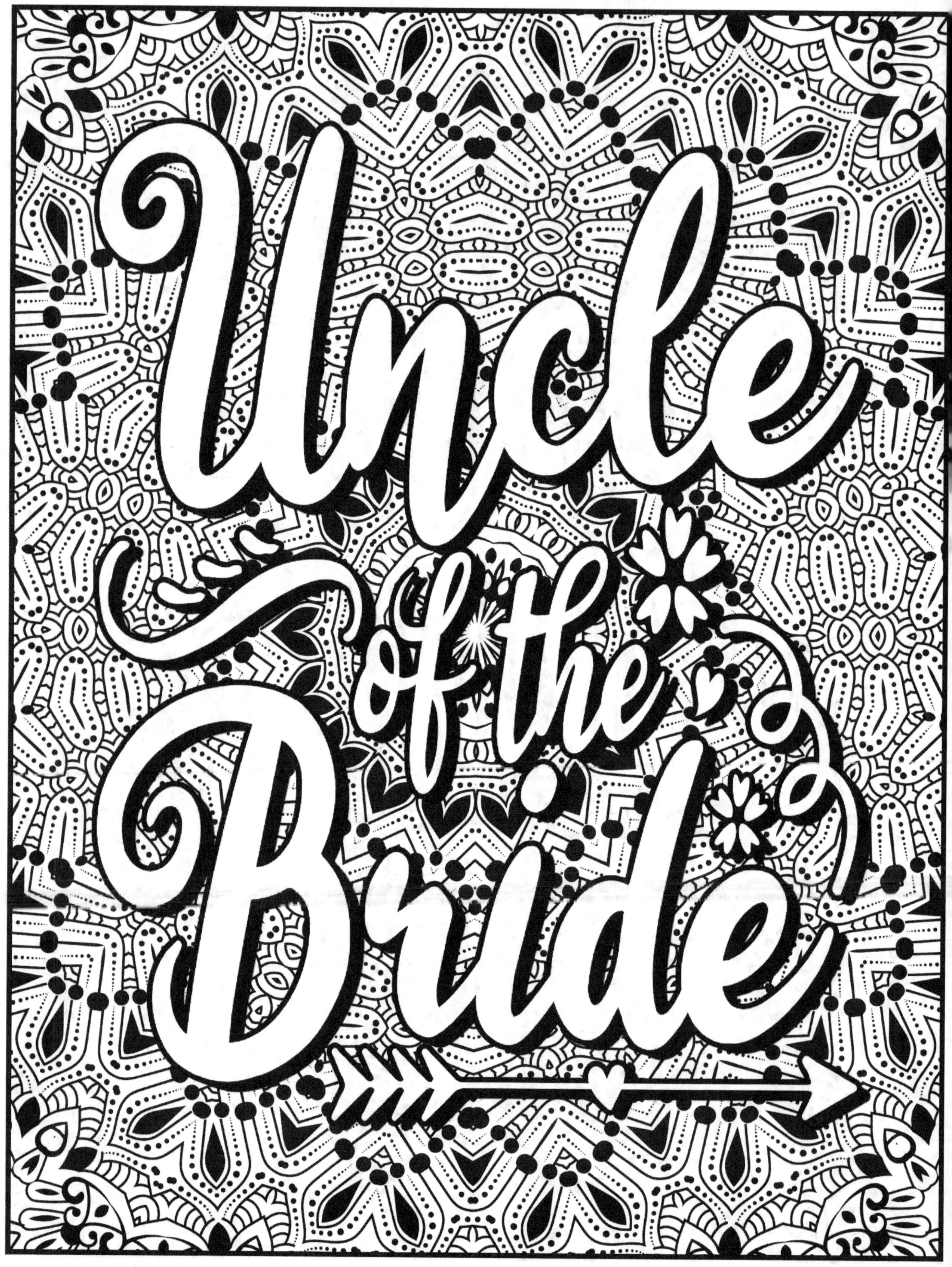

Uncle
of the
Bride

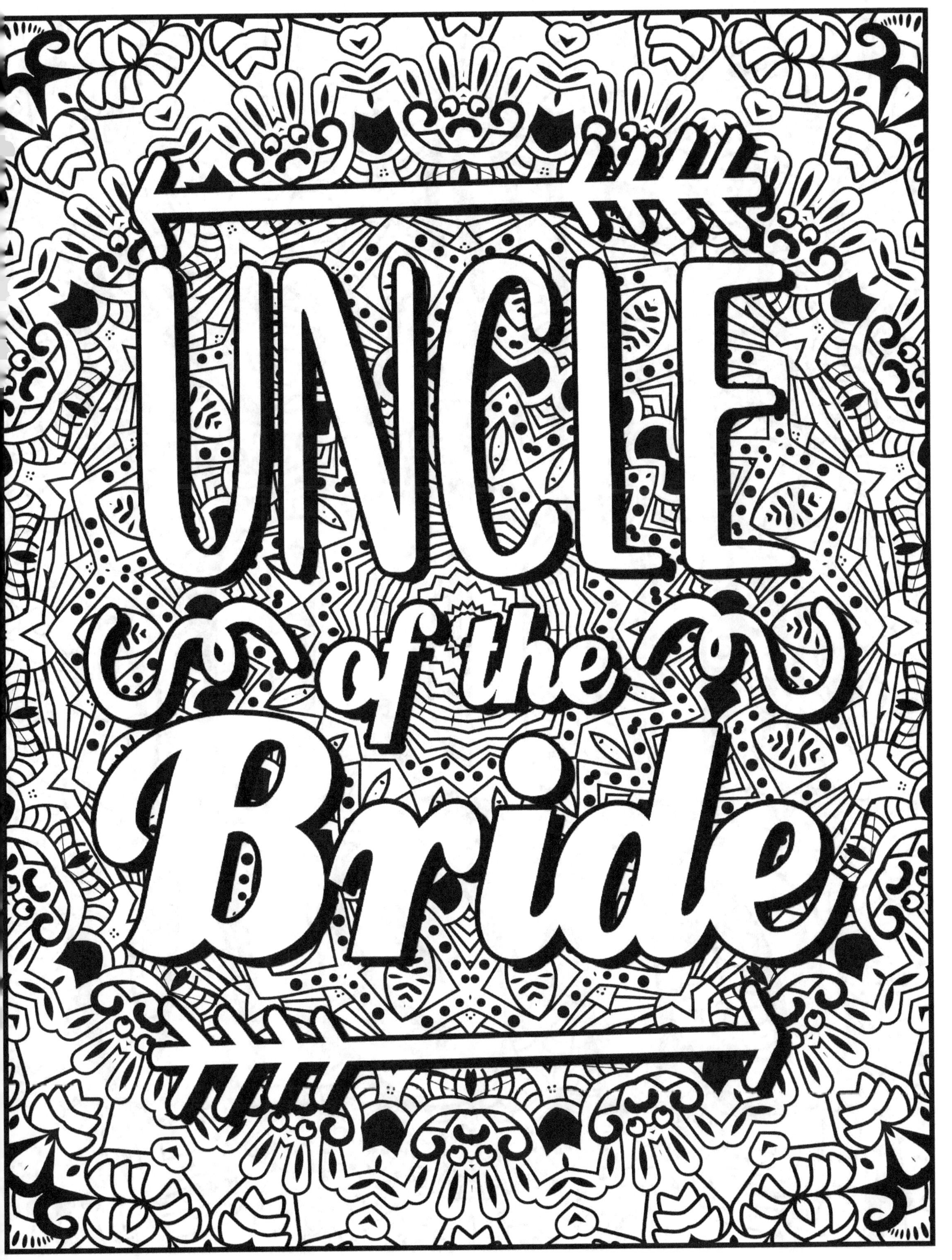

UNCLE
of the
Bride

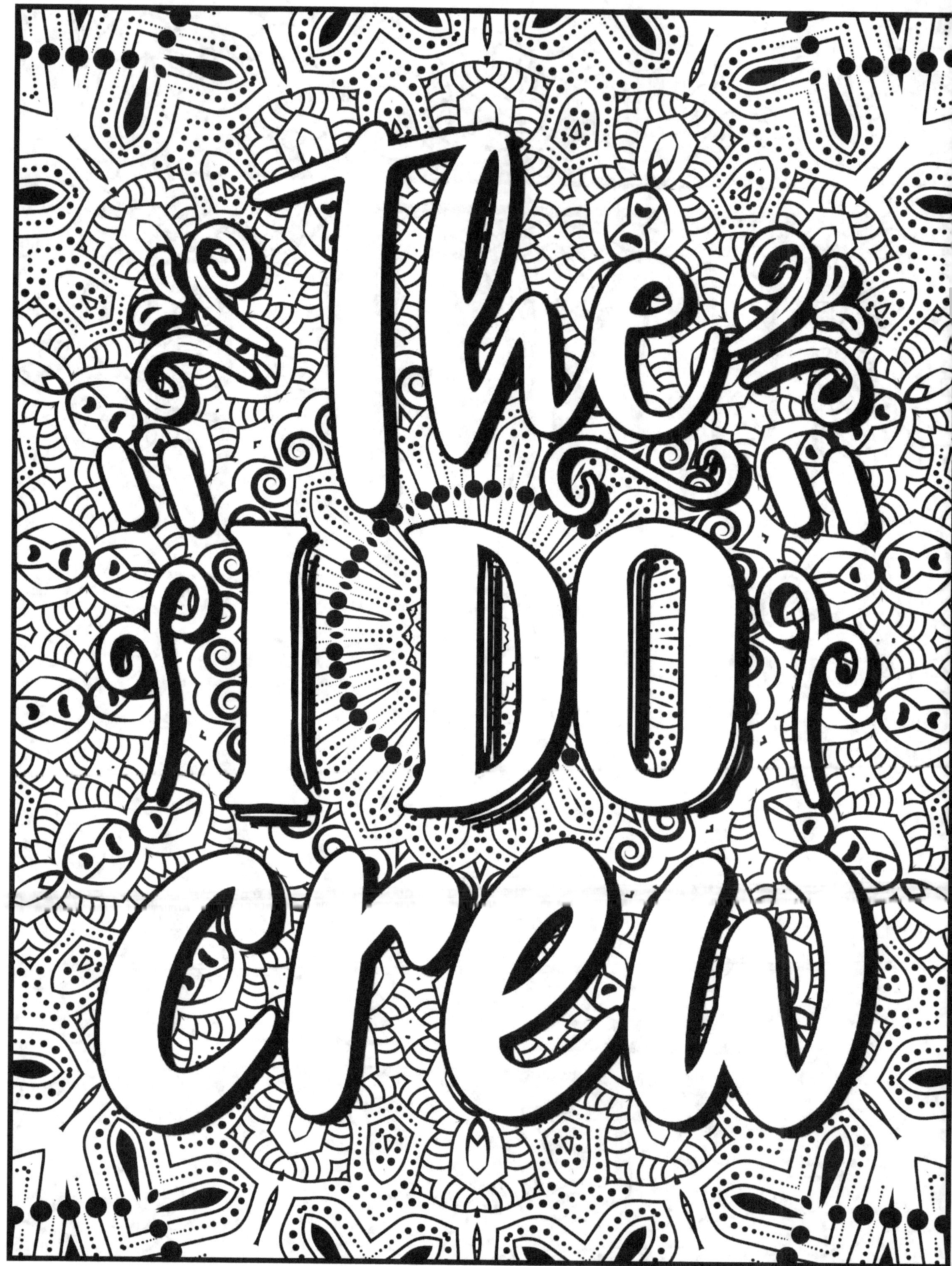

The
"I DO"
crew

Thankful
for my
Tribe

Sweating
for the
wedding

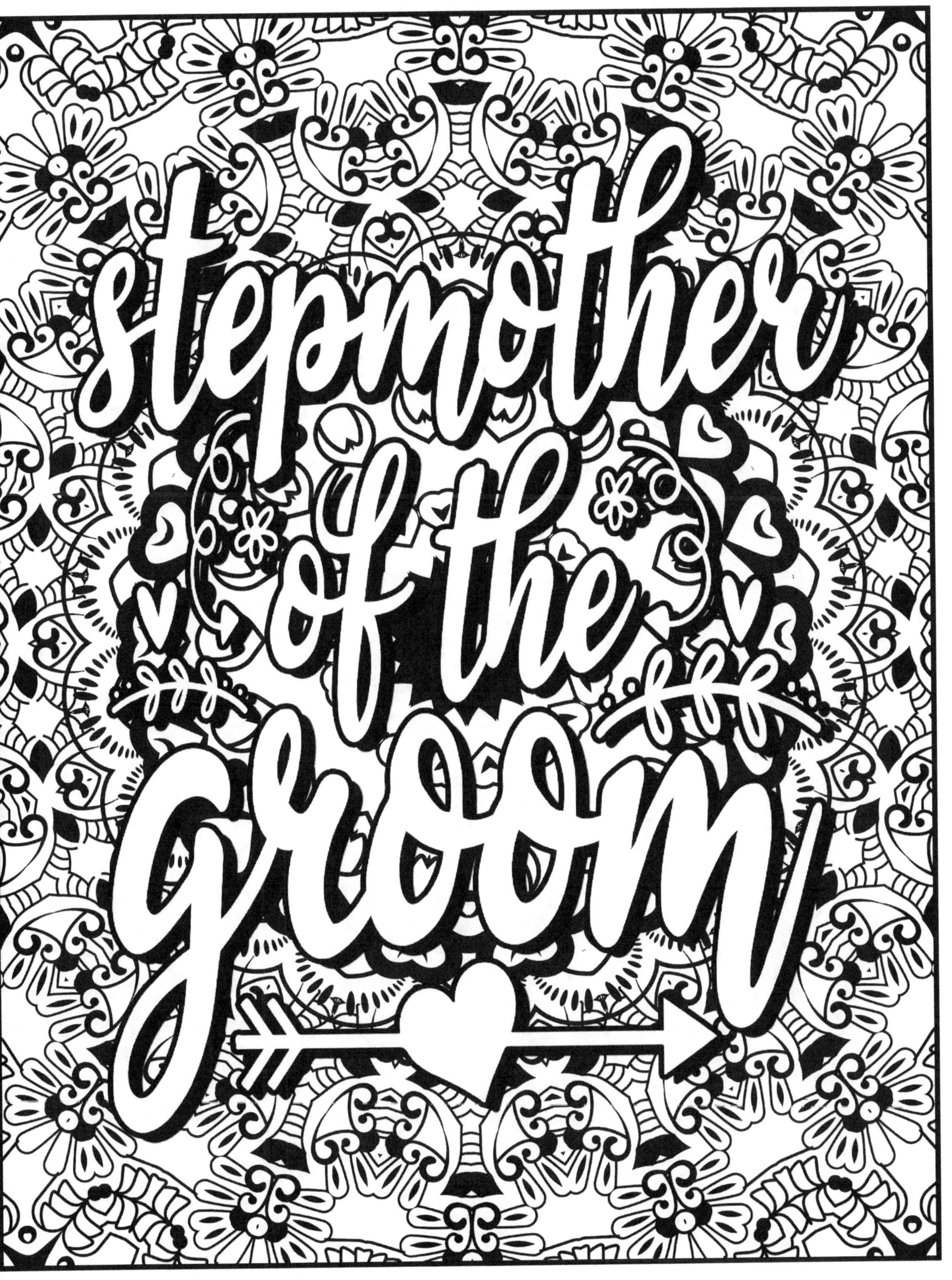

stepmother
of the
groom